Strange Places

Written by Cynthia F. Bergen

2020

Strange Places

Copyright © 2013, 2020 by Cynthia Bergen

All rights reserved. This book or any portion thereof may not be reproduced or used in any manner whatsoever without the expressed written permission of the publisher.

First Printing: 2020

ISBN: 978-0-9970651-3-8

i&R Publishing
https://iandrpublishing.wordpress.com

Ordering Information:
Special discounts are available on quantity purchases by corporations, associations, educators, and others. For details, contact the publisher at the above listed address.

Acknowledgements

Editor
Ajani Abdul-Khaliq

Cover Designer
Emanuel and Will Bermudez

Illustrator
Adam Cordova

Web Creator
Ryan Gernsbacher

Supporting Artists

Jolene Blakely	Denny Archibek	Steve Rodriguez
Gloria Bueno	Anthony Fountain	Raymond Daniel
Isaac Rodriguez	Adam A. Ramirez	Billy Necessary
Dawn Archibek	Aaron Martwick	

Jośe Soria and Vicky Wyman, thank you for your incredible story along with others, the struggles dealing with addiction.

Special thanks to my mother Ruth Woods, The Eternal Light

Strange Places Articles

C47 Houston September/October 2013

La Prensa August 2013

Conexion August 2013

News 29 Fox for Strange Places:
http://youtu.be/c5WY6AJTpS4

Channel 4 WOAI News:
http://youtu.be/c0sFsGQ-vro August 2013

Nick Soulsby, Writer, Strange Places: Indie Art Project Encompassing Visual Written Spheres, January 9, 2015 "I Found My Friends" *The Oral History of Nirvana*.

San Antonio Express-New and MySA.com July 24, 2016.

strangeplacesfilm.com
facebook.com/StrangPlacesFilm.com

Contents

Chapter I 1
Chapter II 5
Chapter III 9
Chapter IV 13
Chapter V 19
Chapter VI 29
Chapter VII 33
Chapter VIII 37
Chapter IX 47
Chapter X 51
Chapter XI 57
Chapter XII 63
Chapter XIII 69

Chapter I

It's nearly 100 degrees outside. Natalie, a 27-year old brunette, sits slouched with heavy eyes as she slowly falls asleep on the bus. Her fatigue defies the actual clock time, as her day is just getting started. Eventually she hears the screeching of the bus brakes, and jostles into shaky alertness. She steps off the bus in an area well known for its restaurants and art. She still has to walk another block.

As she passes by the merchants and their customers, the semi-focused brunette is greeted by several people on the street. "Hello, Natalie!" "Hey Natalie!" "Mornin' Miss Natalie!" One of them even gives her a big hug. Natalie has been working on this strip for at least five years, not too far from her boyfriend who works four blocks down the street. She continues her measured walk into the restaurant where she works and gives dutiful "Hi"s to her co-workers. Watching their black and white waitress uniforms, she hopes no one notices that they are wearing short sleeves while she's wearing long sleeves.

Natalie begins her shift praying against the heavens that she doesn't get the patio. The intense heat out there might rival even the restaurant ovens. Her previous jobs had each been a revolving door, and although she has been at this current job on the strip for three months, there is always the fear of being fired. Before she can prepare herself, her supervisor walks up to her . "Natalie you have section C." She knew it, of course. The patio.

As her first customers arrive, Natalie repeats a practical mantra to herself, hoping its message would magically reach the patrons, *"Please stay inside, not outside."* She obviously gives them the option, to which they fortunately reply, "Inside will do." Natalie is relieved. The next guests are two elderly ladies. Natalie thinks to herself, *"I know they want inside."* To her surprise, though, it's the patio.

Natalie asks the two elderly ladies what they would like to drink. Both want tea. Meanwhile she notices one of the elderly ladies looking around. Natalie informs them that she will return with their drinks. Upon her return a couple of minutes later, however, it becomes clear to Natalie that one of the ladies is studying her. Or maybe not. Natalie tries not to fixate on the feeling by telling herself that she's simply being paranoid. Instead, she asks her guests if they are ready to order. They reply yes, and she does her job as scripted. Once she's done collecting their menus, one of the ladies looks at the server's name tag and finally asks her an overdue question, "Natalie aren't you hot wearing those long sleeves?" Natalie responds, "No Ma'am. I'm anemic and inside is very cold to me." The answer is a satisfactory one, but Natalie's shift has just started. How many more people are going to ask about the long sleeves today? She would think that she might have gotten used to this by now, but that's not so. Her thoughts are soon replaced with a different one that brings a smile to her face. Today is payday for her, and for her boyfriend Miles.

As the day goes on, Natalie occasionally pulls out her cell phone to listen for the dial tone. *Thank God, still on,* she thinks to herself. *Don't forget to pay the cell phone bill.*

Natalie calls up Miles and asks him how his day's been going. "Busy." Natalie then asks if Miles' buddy had come by to see him. The response this time is a chipper "Yup!" which prompts Natalie to change her plans for the day. Excitedly she tells her boyfriend that she'll walk down on her lunch break to see him.

As lunchtime arrives, Natalie isn't so much hungry as she is anxious to see Miles. Immediately upon her arrival, she hurries over to Miles in the kitchen.

Miles, a 35-year-old, 5'9" distinguished looking Hispanic male, has been working at this other restaurant for two years, but is also very familiar with all the venues on this same strip. An accomplished musician, he keeps his popularity high with frequent appearances wherever there are good times to be had. In total, he has worked in the area for about seven years.

Natalie fidgets her feet as she glances impatiently at her watch. In her mind she scolds the boyfriend, *Hurry up Miles! I only have 30 minutes for lunch.* No sooner than she thinks this does she look up towards the rest of the establishment. There's Miles, strolling out of the kitchen. He approaches Natalie and gives her a warm hug. After remaining pressed for a time, Natalie gets down to business and asks Miles for the money to pay the cell phone bill. He reaches in his back pocket and gives Natalie a rolled-up wad of cash. Nervously, Natalie tells Miles that she has to use the bathroom. "Don't go anywhere," she tells him. So Miles waits.

Customers passing Miles offer various friendly gestures, some waving, some patting him on the back, others nodding. Miles is well respected on this strip because he knows, as do others, that a killer chef is hard to find. Upon Natalie's return, Miles asks if she's okay. "Now I am," the brunette smiles. But "Damn it!" Her watch suddenly catches her eye. "It's time for me to go!" The two exchange another hug and Miles resumes his duties as a chef.

Natalie returns to work much more contented than she had been in the morning. Now it doesn't matter if the customers or whoever sit outside on the patio to eat. Even the long sleeves are irrelevant at this point. Who cares if it's hotter than blazes outside? Given her short break just ended, all is right with the world.

Before Natalie realizes it, her day is over. She rapidly proceeds with her normal routine walk back to the restaurant where Miles works, to have a beer and wait for his shift to end. Once there and seated at the bar, Natalie drifts into deep thought, unaware of Miles' stealthy arrival next to her with beer in hand. The boyfriend opens his mouth, slurring his words. Drunk of course, meaning drinking on the job. Natalie inspects the tipsy Miles' face. She is not happy with the sight before her.

"Miles! One of these days they are going to get tired of your shit and fire you! Just like the other jobs!"

Slurring his words some more, Miles answers in a not-so-quiet voice, "They can't. I'm the best fucking chef they have ever had."

Natalie rolls her eyes. "Well hurry up and drink, we don't want to miss the bus."

More dribbling words fall out in a 60-proof cloud, "Come ohn, we never miss thebus."

Miles and Natalie scarf their beer efficiently, then leave holding hands as they head towards to the bus stop.

Chapter II

The two enter their small apartment, Natalie's parents' guest house located in the back of the main house. The unit is adjacent to a two-car garage, where the only room separated from the garage wall is the bathroom. For Natalie and Miles, though, this is more than enough.

As soon as the pair settle down, Natalie notes, "I am going to take a shower first."

"Okay baby," Miles answers with a big seductive smile, "We'll be ready."

Natalie enters the bathroom and closes the door. She takes a moment to strip off her clothes, then looks into the mirror. As she stares at herself, she thinks about how she got where she is. *I still have a cute face I think. Just 28—No. Well, almost—but I feel older. Especially my body.* She remembers how life used to be so much fun when she first met Miles. It was at the club where his band used to play, but not anymore. With all the changes over the years, the only thing that keeps her going now is her love for Miles. She stares into the mirror a little longer before she finally snaps out of it and turns on the shower. She tests the water to make sure temperature is just right.

Natalie wonders why she ever started shaving in the first place. She cuts herself constantly with the blades, and considers that maybe she should just let the hair grow out. Then again, she can't. She needs to keep clean hygiene. Upon entering the shower, she grabs the bar of soap and suds it up, then she reaches for a razor. Beginning at her legs as she rubs the soap; she pulls the blade slowly along. Suddenly there is blood. The red streaks mingle in with the suds as the mixture burns sharply at the cut. Natalie should be used to the pain by now. Even as the running water clears the area, some of the older scabs are now more apparent, their pustules also bleeding in different areas. There is no way to go back in time and uncut them, though. She continues and finishes with the right leg before moving on to the left. It's in the same state. As she rubs the rest of her body, her reason for wearing long sleeves is made even more obvious. The same sores are there on her arms, but greater in number. The stinging soap burns the open sores. The look on Natalie's face tells it all. The pain. *How did I let it go this far? It used to be so much fun!*

Natalie heads to the corner of the room where she and Miles have set up a small round table with two chairs. Some music is playing in the background. Natalie joins Miles who is already sitting down, waiting on her patiently. Natalie takes her seat and carefully rolls up her pants leg. On top of the table are two syringes filled with some black substance.

Miles pulls out a rubber glove from one of his pockets, the same type of glove he uses at work. Next, he stretches out the rubber glove as far as it can be stretched. He then mumbles something to himself.

"What are you mumbling about?" Natalie asks.

"Just thinking to myself how thankful I am for the information my medical student friend gave me for options if no belt or piece of rubber hose is available. A rubber glove works great for a tourniquet."

Miles ties the tourniquet below Natalie's knee cap, and taps a spot so the vein would reveal itself. He takes care not to get too close to the nearby areas that are already hardened and scared from multiple injections. But Natalie has already been overtaken by the urge and is becoming more and more impatient. She starts shaking commands Miles, "Hurry up!"

Chapter II

"Okay! Okay!" Miles taps the area again. Now the vein is visible as it slowly rises up. The boyfriend takes the syringe and holds it with the needle upward. He then tests the syringe by pushing the bottom, causing the black substance to squirt out a little at the needle's tip. "Okay it's ready." He inserts the needle into Natalie's vein and injects.

Natalie closes her eyes.

Once the first syringe is empty, Miles turns to towards a second one prepared for himself. This first gets tossed into a nearby bucket.

Miles, 35 years old, has been doing heroin since he was 16, so at this point it's simply a way of life. Now that the thrill is gone, the injections are a matter of survival. Miles uses heroin three times a day, Natalie two times, where Miles has kept the extra dosage from Natalie. He takes the blame for getting Natalie hooked on this devil of a drug, even though Natalie had mentioned to him that she had used heroin before. She said it was just for recreational purposes. Now neither of them could claim that. Both need it to live. They have tried getting off of it, but the Methadone treatments just didn't give the same high. The cost of black tar heroin, the kind they use, has kept the pair in poverty with its $500 a day price tag. They thank God that Natalie's parents allow them to stay in the guest house rent free.

Natalie had developed a drug problem even before she met Miles. Once her parents learned about it they assisted her in finding a treatment program. That was several years ago, though. As far as they know today, she is clean.

Once Miles has taken his medication, he joins Natalie with closed eyes, as both lose themselves in the mystical music. After an untold amount of time, he listlessly creaks his eyes open again. Natalie remains seated there, focusing on how good life is right now. Good until the feeling for the next fix sets in. Then it starts all over again.

Natalie turns a dazed gaze towards Miles, "You need to call your medical student friend. What's his name?"

Miles answers calmly, "Eric."

"Yeah. Yeah." Thanks to so many needle injections, Natalie has been having problems fighting infections in her legs.

As the night falls, so too do Miles and Natalie collapse into each other's arms.

Chapter III

The following day it's back to work as usual for Miles and Natalie. While at work, Natalie begins to feel a little light headed, though she has only been there for two hours. *Focus*, she tells herself. But having been stuck with the patio again hasn't helped.

As evening approaches, the restaurant entertainment for the day ends up being a belly dancer. While serving, Natalie glances over to the belly dancer and notices, *My god, I went to school with her. Uh, What was her name?...Brittany. That was it.* The name had come instantly. Now getting nervous, Natalie wants to avoid being noticed.

Natalie is trying too hard to stay low key, and while serving a young couple their dinner, she panics wide-eyed as one of the plates slips out of her hands. Luckily it fell on the table and not on the young lady's lap. The couple looks at Natalie, not with anger, but with concern. "I am so sorry," Natalie apologizes pitifully.

"Don't worry, I'm a waitress. It happens," the customer responds.

Natalie does not know that she's been seen by one of her coworkers, who stealthily disappears into the back. Natalie continues to apologize while she cleans up the mess. Suddenly she turns around to see the manager headed her way.

The unamused frame walks right by the anxious server and starts talking to the guests. He apologizes for the incident, then turns an iron glare towards Natalie. "You don't look so well. Why don't you clock out NOW, and go home and get some rest." As he speaks, Natalie glances towards the young lady at the table just in time to read her lips, "Ass-hole," the customer points a mocking but hidden finger to the manager. Natalie has to fight to hold back a laugh. *Have to pay attention.* Instead, all she can say in response is, "Okay I will do that."

But the escape from work isn't as simple as that. As Natalie nears the time clock, she spots her friend from school, Brittany. The entertainer is still a little out of breath from performing, but announces with excitement, "I knew that was you causing all that trouble over there! Just like in school. Natalie, how are you?"

"I'm okay. Just been a long day, so I'm going home to get some rest."

"Yeah you don't look so hot, but we need to get together soon and talk about old times. I live in Austin but had a gig here. So there's a possibility I'll be back again. But let me give you my number. Do you have your cell with you?"

Natalie fumbles around for her phone, hoping to end the awkwardly timed meeting as quickly as possible.

Brittany gives Natalie her number. "Got it!" the tired server announces in the most interested voice possible.

"Okay girl take care! I would hug you but I'm sweaty," Brittany explains.

Natalie forces a smile. "Okay, I'd better clock out before my boss thinks I'm stealing from the company."

"I understand."

Natalie heads straight to the time clock to punch out, noticing one of the waitresses staring at her in the process. *I know she's the snitch.*

Chapter III

Natalie pulls out her cell phone again. It's dead of course. She had only pretended to save Brittany's number. But *Damn!* she thinks to herself. *Forgot about the bill. Miles is working the late shift tonight, so he should be ready right now to catch the bus to work. So what's going to happen here?*

Miles' and her busses pass each other. She could walk down to the restaurant where he works and tell one of his co-workers that she had gone home. But that doesn't happen. Instead, Natalie decides to stay put and wait for her own bus.

Sometime later she arrives home.

Hesitantly, she closes the front door behind her.

Chapter IV

Just before getting off the bus, Miles tries to call Natalie. Realizing the phone is dead, he thinks to himself, *Damn it, Natalie! I thought you were going to pay the cell phone bill!* Now as he considers it some more, he comes closer to frustration. *This situation has to stop. We are not getting anywhere in our lives.*

Yet again it happens. Miles quickly makes his drug deal in the restroom, then mosies back into the restaurant kitchen.

While on break Miles glances at his watch. It's almost 9:00pm. The phone is disconnected, but why didn't Natalie stop by at her lunch break? Concern begins to creep in. *She'd never miss the injection for her daily fix,* he admits to himself.

After his shift, Miles heads to the bus stop. He doesn't have to wait long before seeing it already heading his way.

I haven't seen her at all today. What the hell happened to her? Once back home, though, his spirit brightens a little as he pulls open the screen door. He puts the key into the lock. She must be waiting for him. But the knob turns with no resistance.

Wait a minute, Miles worries even more than before, *Natalie knows better. She is to keep this door locked at all times.* It doesn't matter that they are behind her parents' house. Entering the front door Miles yells, "Natalie!"

No Natalie in sight. The TV isn't even on.

"Natalie!"

Miles finally makes his way towards the bathroom, only to find his beloved next door in the bedroom on the floor. There she lay beside the bed, her body jerking violently from head to toe. "Natalie!" Miles screeches in panic, immediately getting down on his knees and holding her. "Natalie!" Miles pleads. "Baby you're having a seizure."

Natalie has had seizures in the past, but this one is different. It's clearly more severe. "I'm going to call EMS," Miles grabs for his phone. But he and Natalie have already had this talk before. No hospitals. Especially with them living with her parents and risking them seeing ambulances at their house. Natalie had told her parents she was clean, not doing drugs anymore. But Miles knows that she could die without immediate attention.   With the cell phone being turned off, using her parents' phone is out of the question. *Urgh,* Miles growls half-frustrated, half-afraid. "NEED A PHONE!" But the closest convenience store is two blocks away. "Baby. Baby. I am going to get help." He pulls a pillow from the bed and puts it under her head. She is not jerking as much as before by the time Miles makes it outside.

Miles had never asked whether the convenience store even *had* a pay phone, since everyone has a cell except for him right now. "Damn it! Damn it!" Miles shouts out loud, "NATALIE YOU SHOULD HAVE PAID THE BILL!" But now is not the time to be angry. Immediately he begins pointing to himself. *I know I am mostly to blame.* Finally making it to the store, Miles luckily spots a pay phone. Thanking God for the old technology. He digs in his pockets for the correct change, then decides to call his medical student friend Eric instead of EMS. The problem is, he doesn't have Eric's number memorized. It's on his cell phone.

"Fucking technology!" *Wait a minute. I still should be able to pull up my contact list.* Seconds later he's found it. *Yes! Got It! Eric's number.*

Chapter IV

He dials it and waits.

Miles gets Eric's voice mail. *Shit! He won't answer if he doesn't recognize the number.* Miles waits a little longer for the chance to leave a message. Following the beep, he sprays a panicked jumble of words into the phone. "Eric this is Miles, I'm at a pay phone, call me back at this number. I have an emergency, it's Natalie. She's having a seizure." Miles hangs up and waits some more for the call back. Meanwhile, he searches his pockets again for more change, only to find only two quarters. But the price for a call is eighty cents.

Now he has to go find some change. *But do I leave the phone? What if it rings while I'm away from it? What if he doesn't check the message? What if I can't get him? Who else could help?* Still waiting by the phone. Nothing. Miles glances at the silent phone. Then the store. Then the phone again. He desperately scans the ground for change someone might have dropped. Or someone around that he could ask. It's just 30 cents. *But the one person there getting gas…No.* Another desperate gaze at the phone. Then the store. Finally he hurries towards the front door of the store when suddenly he hears the pay phone ring. Quickly he runs back to it.

Yanking the receiver to his ear, Miles barks, "Eric!"

There is a slight pause before the voice on the other end replies. "No, who's this?" it drawls confusedly, "Uh, can I speak to Suzanne?"

Miles is enraged, "GET OFF THIS FUCKING LINE!!" he slams down the receiver. Now disoriented, Miles feels uncontrollably dizzy as he backs away from the pay phone. Suddenly he turns around to a pair of blinding headlights backed by the screeching of tires. Miles is stiff as future roadkill.

The driver jumps out of the car and yells at Miles, "Are you out of your mind! Get in!" Eric orders Miles. "You are a lucky man. I was just in the area on my way out of town, but when I got your message hauled ass. The whole block must have seen you yelling at that phone."

Eric and Miles quickly arrive back at the house and hurry straight through the front door. Natalie had somehow managed to work her way toward the wall, banging her head against it. Eric announces immediately, "We are going to have to take her to the emergency room."

Miles' face turns white with fear. He knows Natalie would rather die. They had discussed this. She didn't want people to know their business. How seriously she'd be judged. They'd look down upon her as just another drug addict. And everyone will know. Still, unhesitantly Eric gathers up Natalie in his arms and directs Miles, "Get the door." Miles' concerns now shifts towards Natalie's parents. If they were to appear right now it would be all over. He hopes they have dozed off in front of the TV, maybe blinded by a movie, or stuffed with popcorn.

Eric walks far ahead of Miles towards the car which had been left parked in front of the next-door neighbors' house. The jerking and twitching of Natalie's body won't stop as he stands waiting for Miles to open the door to the back seat. Eric tells Miles to get in the back seat, which Miles does, then the medical student carefully lowers Natalie in with her head resting on Miles' lap. Miles immediately puts his arms around his girlfriend and holds her twitching body as Eric closes the door.

Eric questions Miles, "Okay Miles I know you guys don't have hospital insurance."

"No we don't."

Eric continues, "I am going to take you to the county hospital where they will take care of you. That's also where I am doing my internship."

"But won't they notice you Eric?"

"First of all, I'm here in the daytime. Plus, you are going to carry her in, not me. I don't want to risk my nursing career." Eric knows this may have been harsh to say, but knowing that your friend is a heroin addict...He's preached to Miles 1000 times before; now it has come to this. Miles, on the other hand, is listening to everything, endless thoughts flooding through his mind. *This is what Natalie tried to avoid—people knowing about our addiction, passing judgement.* But Miles again realizes that he doesn't blame them. He is definitely to blame.

Chapter IV

This is all my fault.

Eric pulls his car up to the ER entrance, where an ambulance already sits in wait for other critical situations like theirs. Eric gets out and opens the car door for Miles. "Go in and get a nurse and tell them she is having a seizure. I'll stay here with her."

With Natalie still seizing, Miles quickly returns with two nurses with a stretcher in tow. As soon as Natalie is loaded onto the stretcher, Miles closes the back car door. Eric, without even saying goodbye, drives off as a stranger to the young couple. Despite the necessary distance, however, the medical student does manage to look through the rearview mirror with a thought to himself, *Good luck my friend.*

Chapter V

The medical staff move Natalie to triage to determine the severity of her situation. Miles can only sit fidgeting in the waiting room, occasionally getting up to pace around before taking his seat again. He doesn't know what to expect. Suddenly they call his name; immediately he hurries over to the patient information desk for the verdict.

Miles sits down quietly in one of the two chairs in front of the clerk. The stone-faced middle-aged lady methodically collects Natalie's information, eventually arriving at the part about insurance.

"Mr. Gonzales does your friend Natalie have any insurance?"

Eric had warned him about this. "No ma'am," Miles answers nervously.

"How about you sir?" the clerk continues, unmoved by Miles' first answer.

Miles' response is the same. "No Ma'am."

The clerk continues her typing.

In the corner of his eye, Miles sees one of the nurses who had taken Natalie to the back. He studies her lips as her low, monotone voice mixes in with the rest of the background noise. "Due to...tensive heroin use, multiple vei...ar tissue," she told a colleague. "An IV specialist...take a stab at it?" The two staff members then disappear around a corner, out of Miles sight. Miles once again repeats to himself, "See this is what Natalie wanted to avoid. Hopefully my baby didn't hear this." Soon Miles finishes giving the clerk his and Natalie's information, and is asked to take a seat once again. No real news yet. He'll just have to wait until they call him, and that won't happen until she has been moved to a room.

One hour. Two hours. Three hours. Four. Miles is out of his mind with impatience, and gets up to ask the new clerk what the deal is. The old clerk had long finished her shift.

"Ma'am I have been waiting for hours."

"The patient's name?" the clerk asked.

"Natalie Ortiz."

"Just a second sir."

The clerk goes in the back to check. After a while, she returns with an update. "Sir, Ms. Ortiz is being transported into a room right now. She'll be located…"

Chapter V

Miles only half hears the instructions for how to find the main elevators to the patient's rooms.

"Thank you," Miles told her aloud, but under his breath a stream of curses poured out. It's a good thing he had asked. Otherwise he would have still been sitting there.

The hospital is a ghost town. Miles locates the elevator and rushes right in as soon as the doors open. He gets off the elevator on the floor whose sign reads "Medical Surgical." Following the room, passing door after door, forking hallway after forking hallway, he eventually stops at a nurses station. Behind the counter sits a very petite young lady typing on the computer. Miles, by now, is exhausted.

"Excuse me, I was just told my friend was moved to this floor?"

"Can I have her name sir?"

"It's Natalie Ortiz."

The young clerk looks up the name on the computer then turns around and checks the patient's board. Miles searches the board as well, but doesn't see Natalie's name.

The clerk turns to Miles with a slight frown. "Sir we don't have a patient by that name."

Miles is too tired to throw a tantrum. Gingerly he explains to the girl, "I was just in the emergency room and they said she was en route to this floor."

The young lady, who must be the unit clerk, senses that Miles is about to lose it. "Let me check with ER," she replies.

The clerk makes a call down to ER, and gives them Natalie's name. Miles watches her intently while she nods her head up and down. Finally she hangs up the phone. "Okay Mr. Ortiz—"

That's not my last name. but right now who cares.

"—she was redirected to the intensive care unit."

"ICU!?" Miles reacts with loud frustration.

But the unit clerk has seen this kind of response more times than she can count. Politely she gives Miles directions to ICU, and assures him that she's being taken care of there. "...down on the second floor Sir." Before she can say anything else to him, however, Miles is gone.

She was going to tell him that visiting hours are at 9:00am. Right now it's 5:50am.

As Miles takes the elevator down to the Intensive Care Unit he thinks, *All this for drugs!* Soon after, as the elevator doors open, he sees the nurses station right in front of him. Thank God it wasn't a mile away.

Miles rushes to the front desk, where an older lady in scrubs sits perched and on guard. By the look of it, she must be a nurse.

"Excuse me, I am looking for Natalie Ortiz," Miles huffs.

The nurse inspects the distraught man. Rather than asking if this Natalie person is a patient, she gets straight to the point instead. "Sir, just to let you know, visiting hours start at 9am." She is polite, but firm.

Miles glances at the clock behind the lady. It shows 6am. The irritated man is suddenly overcome with disappointment, but is too tired to cause a scene.

Soothingly the nurse continues, "Let me check first to see if she is here."

Miles can only nod his head in defeat.

As Miles waits patiently for the nurse to locate Natalie, he glimpses a nurse not too far away pushing a stretcher. On the stretcher lies a patient partially covered with a sheet, causing Miles to begin panicking immediately. *What if that's Natalie?* Miles muscles' refuse to move as his frozen gaze drifts closer to the patient's face. *OH MY GOD!*

Chapter V

"—ir we do have Ms. Ortiz here, but like I said visiting hours start at 9am." Miles hasn't realized that the nurse behind the desk has been talking to him. "We do have a waiting room through the double doors to the right."

Miles comes to his senses. "Is she going to be okay?"

The question is part of the normal routine for the nurse. People are always claiming to be related to the patient, always upset for one reason or another—more from not knowing than for any of their initial reasons alone. She adds, "All I can tell you is that she's in good hands. You look very tired. Why don't you go home and relax, or just wait in our waiting room?

Miles barely has enough energy to nod his head. "Thank you," he tells the nurse.

Miles now remembers that he was driven to the hospital. Now he tries to decide what to do. Does he take the bus or just stay? But to him this is a no brainer. It would take a total of three hours back and forth on the bus. Might as well stay.

Miles' thoughts, for the most part, remain on Natalie during his stay in the waiting room. Suddenly, however, they switch to the patient being transported on the stretcher. She was a female, brunette just like Natalie, but on her forehead…a blackened hole the size of a quarter. Had she been shot? Maybe she was shot, but wouldn't she be dead? *Why is she in ICU?* Miles tries several times to shake the thoughts from his head, but with little success. Finally after such a long night, the beleaguered boyfriend dozes off, an uneasy scowl fixed on his face.

Suddenly a loud CRASH causes Miles to jump from his sleep. He's been dreaming about the accident that he and Natalie survived that left their vehicle totaled. They were lucky to escape death. His eyes dart around, confused and incoherent. His heart races as he nervously pulls together scattered thoughts, the foreignness of his whereabouts and icy cold of the room shaking him even further. *Where am I?* Miles looks at his watch. It is now 8:30am.

Miles isn't alone in the room. Another young couple sits some distance off in the corner. Surveying some more, he soon spots a vending machine. One that sells coffee, no less. Somewhat relieved, he heads over to the machine and reaches in his pockets for $2.00. But of course, there was only 50 cents, remember? Miles lets his head thump against the machine, leaning on it for a while with his palm against the display window. He breathes slowly, deeply in resignation. A few seconds later, the young man of the couple in the corner approaches the machine and inserts $2.00. He briefly taps Miles' shoulder and heads back to his seat. Miles turns a weary eye just long enough to give a groggy, "Thanks." The young man doesn't turn around, but does nod his head in acknowledgement.

As Miles sits down with his coffee, he wonders if last night was just a dream. No, probably a nightmare. Reality gradually sinks in.

9:00am comes and Miles enters the double doors as he did four hours earlier. It's straight to the nurses station, where a different person now sits behind the desk. This one is middle aged but petite, also wearing scrubs. She looks up and asks Miles, "May I help you?"

"Yes, I am here to see Natalie Ortiz."

The nurse searches the name on the computer, then replies to an anxious Miles, "She's in bed 5, but visiting is only 30 minutes."

Miles nods his head up and down mechanically.

Following the ICU signs, then the signs for ICU beds, Miles walks through another set of double doors. So many beds are there, most surrounded by curtains for privacy. Miles assumes that the beds start on the righthand side. He begins counting beds on his way through, but as he gets closer to bed 5 he hears a sudden click and slam against the floor behind him.

A nurse has dropped her chart.

Miles sighs heavily, so tired of surprises, before turning back towards his goal.

Chapter V

Finally, bed 5. Miles ducks into the curtain to see Natalie. Fright washes over him at the shock of what he sees. He steps back quickly, trembling a little.

"Sir Miss Ortiz is in the next bed, bed 5," the nurse standing behind him advises.

Clearly this one isn't her. It's the lady with the hole in her forehead. Miles backs up cautiously, the image burned into his brain as his face struggles to regain its color.

Miles approaches the next curtain carefully. Natalie should be behind it, but after what he's just seen, he's not sure anymore. Pulling back the barrier, he finally discovers his beloved Natalie lying there, sleeping peacefully. The nurse Miles had just run into now took her position behind a monitor. This is, after all, ICU.

"We had to insert the IV in her neck," the nurse explains. "Her veins collapsed because of such heavy usage."

Miles gets the message.

Still standing at the foot of the bed, the nurse glances at Natalie and then back at Miles. "You can go ahead and hold her hand, it's okay!"

"She's been sleeping and it seems the seizing has passed. But we are keeping her under observation," the nurse continues. "And sir, as a reminder, you only have 30 minutes."

Miles shakes his head as he stares at Natalie, partly relieved, partly concerned, but mostly at a loss for thoughts. With a chair already posted by the bed, Miles gingerly walks over and sits down, proceeding to hold Natalie's hand. Immediately Natalie stirs, slowly opens her eyes with a weak smile, then lets her eyelids fall again. Miles smiles back with excitement, just in time for his beloved to see him perhaps. Soon her eyes are completely closed again.

The seizing probably took a lot out of her. And I guess she's been heavily sedated... Miles thinks to himself. *Speaking of heavy sedation, I could sure use some about now.*

Visitation time flies by. 10 minutes have already gone by and 20 minutes remain. Miles sits calmly by Natalie's side for what seems like only a few seconds longer. Suddenly he hears voices from the other side of the curtain. They are coming from around the bed of the lady with the hole in her forehead. Miles can't help but listen.

"Has she woken up at all?" A man's voice asks one of the nurses. Miles figures this must be the doctor.

"No doctor, I think she really did it this time. She missed the vein in her forehead, but with the heroin she injected causing that abscess…"

Miles is shocked. *This time? THIS TIME!? Apparently she's a regular.* Panic settles on Miles' face. *She has been shooting heroin in her forehead!?* Miles never knew there was a vein there. What a strange place.

After a few more minutes, Miles hears another voice over his shoulder. "Sir."

Miles turns around. It's the nurse.

"Sir, visiting time is over. The next visiting time is at 3pm."

Chapter V

With a look of bottled despair, Miles acknowledges the nurse. As she leaves to tend to the next patient, Miles continues to hold Natalie's hand, bending over to give her a kiss on the cheek. He closes his eyes and kisses her softly, slowly opening his eyes to leave. One last look at his beloved, Miles shakes in shock. It's not Natalie, but the lady with the hole in her forehead. He cries out in horror and abruptly opens his eyes, dropping the cold claw of a hand back on the bed as he reels back from the chair. Yet Natalie peers at him with a half alert curiosity. It was only his imagination playing tricks on him. Considering the lack of sleep, it's probably understandable. As his own eyes adjust, Natalie closes hers once again. Maybe she sensed the kiss, or maybe she had just come out of a nice dream.

As Miles leaves Natalie's bedside, he has to pass by that lady again. Looking at her fills him with dread, but not looking at her...isn't really an option. The giant rotting hole in her head is still there. She's still there. Just lying there motionless.

Now exiting the hospital, Miles thinks about whether or not he should go to work. *I could take a quick nap on the bus and go straight to work now, or go home and take a much needed shower. Then lay down for 30 minutes and...and DON'T miss the bus.* He decides to go home.

Sometime later, Natalie opens her eyes, finally waking in earnest. She tries to focus on her whereabouts, but all she can see is white. Soon she realizes where she is. It was the last thing she wanted. She had told Miles, NO. HOSPITALS!! But it's too late now.

Chapter VI

Miles awakens in a dizzy spin, weak and confused as he fumbles for the clock. "Oh no! 4:00pm!" He curses out loud. "Oh shit! I was supposed to be at work at 1:00!"

Miles has already been given warnings about being late to work, and a more serious warning regarding his occasional no-show, but lately he has been arriving on time and his attendance has been much better. Until now. Miles hurries out of the apartment, down to the corner store. It's hard to believe he was just here yesterday, frantically calling Eric. Now he is frantically calling his job. He asks to speak to his supervisor, Darin.

Whoever initially answered the phone gets back on the line after a brief hold, and tells Miles that Darin isn't in. Miles gradually recognizes the voice. He doesn't know the guy by name, but always refers to him simply as "asshole." Miles asks the guy, "Could you please do me a favor?"

The asshole on the phone replies, "Sure!"

—which doesn't sound believable to Miles. "This is Miles, and I will not be in due to an emergency," he explains (even though he should have been there 3 hours ago). "If he needs to get in touch with me, have me paged at the Community Hospital in ICU."

The asshole on the phone answers as if nothing major has changed, "Alrighty, take care," and hangs up.

Miles arrives at the hospital and heads directly to the ICU floor. Immediately he is distracted by a gurney with a patient on it, fully covered under a white sheet. Miles waits for them to pass, then proceeds straight to Natalie's bed. A quick glance at his watch shows that it's 6:00pm on the dot. He feels much more refreshed now after taking a nap and a well needed shower, so that he now travels the halls as one on a mission. Miles approaches the curtain and enters, only to find *no Natalie!* Miles' eyes widen. He panics for a moment, then quickly remembers the patient he had just seen being wheeled out on the gurney. "Oh my God!" Miles says with a gasp. He leaves the area suddenly, knowing he needs to find the patient that they were taking away.

Miles spots the transporters waiting for the elevator. Without thinking he quickly approaches the gurney and pulls back the white sheet. At the sight before him, his face transforms from disturbed to disfigured, from disfigured to disgusted. It's the lady with the hole in her forehead. The two transporters look at Miles curiously. "Is this a family member?" one of them asks.

Miles takes a while to regain his bearings after seeing the patient who had died. He shakes his head "no" in a daze, barely noticing that the transporters are talking to him.

"Well that's a good thing. Man they are going to have to do one serious makeover on that head," one of the men comments.

"Yeah!" the other replies. "I heard she was a prostitute and a user. Shot her shit in her head, missed the vein, then it got infected. Now here she is."

The elevator opens. "Here we go." One of the transporters politely turns to Miles, "Ah, sir would you mind?" Miles realizes he still has the sheet in his hand. Somewhat embarrassed, he carefully covers the patient back up.

Chapter VI

"Thanks man." The two get into the elevator and the door closes in front of them. Miles remains at the elevator.

"Rest in peace."

Now Miles' thoughts shift. Where the hell is Natalie? Without any further ideas, he returns to the ICU nurses station. This time a very young lady sits behind the computer. Miles braces himself, trying to keep his composure.

"Excuse me, I am looking for the patient that was in bed 5?"

"Her name sir?"

"Natalie Ortiz."

The young lady types quickly, and soon has the information. "She was moved to Medical Surgical on the 8th floor."

Feeling relieved, Miles thanks the clerk. Before she can reply with a "you're welcome," Miles is already headed back to the elevators.

The nurse checking Natalie's vital signs addresses the patient optimistically, "Well hello there. Glad to see you're awake." Natalie tries to focus, but everything is fuzzy. "Everything looks great! They'll be bringing your dinner really soon. You might not want to eat; that's normal for now. But what I need for you to do is drink plenty of fluids and urinate in this container."

Natalie lies there still, and turns her head halfway away from the nurse. *The nurse knows I'm a addict! Damn it Miles!* Natalie then feels her neck, where they have inserted the IV. Suddenly she knows why. Right behind Natalie's nurse stands Miles. He startles Natalie with his appearance on her blind side, but manages a happy "Hi!"

"You're just in time. She just woke up," the nurse comments. She then turns back to Natalie. "My name is Nancy. I will be your nurse so, if you need anything just push this button right here and I will come a running. I will be back shortly to give you your meds."

Natalie nods in reluctant acknowledgement.

As soon as the nurse leaves, Natalie throws a defiant glare at Miles, "You fucking asshole. I told you no hospitals! I told you! I TOLD you!" Natalie, though still very weak, nevertheless has enough strength to be livid. Miles can only feel confused. Given everything he's been through in the last 24 hours, this is the thanks he gets.

Miles can't do anything other than love Natalie, especially now, but at this moment his head hangs low as if the life has been knocked out of him. He loves her so much, but somehow, more than that, he's suddenly overcome with a sense of powerlessness, feeling very, very sad. Natalie continues yelling, each curse getting louder and louder.

Miles can barely get a word in, "But Natalie, Natalie you're alive!"

Natalie continues her tirade, "I told you! I told you! Now they all know!" The angry young lady grabs a cup of water which the nurse had poured for her, and flings the whole thing at Miles, a paper cup and a splash of purified drink landing against his face. Immediately the nurse reappears.

"Sir, I'm sorry but I am going to have to ask you to leave."

Miles departs without a word, drenched.

Nancy turns back to Natalie. "Okay, you are going to have to calm down." Now with medications in hand, she then administers them to the hyperventilating young woman. Shortly thereafter, the nurse returns to her other tasks.

Finding herself alone in a room with one more empty bed, Natalie is still angry, but grateful there are no roommates. In a sudden smash of fatigue, she dozes off.

Chapter VII

Natalie quickly awakens to the sound of conversation. At first they seem like voices in a dream, though soon she realizes they are coming from the other side of the curtain, now drawn closed. Apparently she now has a roommate. From what Natalie can tell, there are more people than just the patient there. Two, three, maybe four people are behind the curtain, at least a couple of them in their early 20s judging by the slang they use. Soon a more mature voice enters the scene.

"Ladies if you can step out for a second, I need to talk to Dee."

The neighboring bed quiets down, leaving only the latest voice, probably that of the nurse.

The nurse speaks softly to Dee. "You are eight months pregnant."

"Yes! Or that's what they told me."

"You are here because your blood count is as low as it is, combined with your usage of drugs."

Natalie tries to keep quiet, but gasps instinctively. She wonders if they heard her. *Eight months pregnant and using!*

"Whatever," Dee responds.

The Nurse continues, "Well, we are going to be administering blood to you in the next hour. We are checking to see if we have your blood type available."

There is no answer from Dee.

"I'll be back shortly."

Seconds later, Dee's friends are back in the room. *Hope I don't have to use the restroom,* Natalie thinks to herself. Because the bathroom is located on Dee's side of the room, the only thing that is close by is the wash basin, in the center of the room. There, however, a man in scrubs appears, washing his hands. Natalie notices he is looking in the mirror not at her, but at Dee's side of the room, glancing over his shoulder to the right. *What's he looking at? Maybe one of the young ladies? What a perv.*

Natalie hears one of the young ladies tell Dee, "Okay girl we have to go. Have fun and enjoy!"

But how can you have fun and enjoy in a hospital, especially when you're pregnant? Natalie wonders.

As soon as the girls leave, the guy in the scrubs leaves too! Natalie wonders off and on for a while what was he staring at.

In a matter of minutes Natalie can see a little through the mirror, that the guy in the scrubs and the nurse are back in the room. Yet the voice that she hears is not the guy's or the nurse's, but that of a third person—a male of high authority. Something is going down.

The authority begins talking to Dee. "Ma'am would you mind if we take a look under your mattress." He gives one of those requests which might as well be a command.

Dee's voice is laced with protest, "Why?"

The man replies, "We believe there could be illegal activity going on."

Natalie, upon hearing the tone of voice, suddenly freezes.

Chapter VII

"I don't know what you're talking about," Dee denies. "No!"

The of authority voice, which Natalie now believes belongs to a cop, repeats his request. "I am going to ask you again, if we could look underneath your mattress."

Dee clearly has had second thoughts. "Yes you may." The neighboring bed is quiet for a while.

"Is this yours?"

Dee replies nervously, but indignantly, "No sir!"

"I heard you had visitors?"

"Yes sir."

Now Natalie knows for certain that he is a cop. With a better look in the mirror, her guess is confirmed. Next to him stands the guy in scrubs, who suddenly looks into the mirror and catches Natalie prying. He briefly returns eye contact then pulls back the curtain, blocking Natalie's view. Natalie is embarrassed, knowing she's been caught eavesdropping. She just couldn't help but stare. She still can't help but listen.

The cop continues, "Did your friends put this under your mattress?"

"No sir."

"Do you know what this is?"

"No sir."

"This is black tar heroin."

Chapter VIII

Miles gazes out through the window of the bus, wondering what just happened. With all the love he has for Natalie… Now she's pushing him away. The bus ride is a blur while Miles reflects. *There's no Natalie to go home to. It's only 7:30pm but… Might as well go to work. Maybe that will take my mind off of her.* The way he feels right now, not even a quick fix of heroin could ease him. Even though he has some on him.

Miles pulls the syringe partway from his pocket and looks at it, thinking about what has transpired within the past 24 hours. *If this is a dream, I'm ready to wake up.*

Miles walks into the kitchen just in time to run into his supervisor Darin. "Hey, is everything okay?" Darin asks. "I got your message."

Miles answers, "Yes, decided to come in."

"Great! You want to take over cutting these tomatoes? I need to go and finish payroll."

"Sure!"

Darin hands Miles the knife and leaves.

As he cuts the tomatoes, Miles struggles to shake off the past 24 hours. Now he wishes he had just gone home. Right behind Miles stands the coolheaded co-worker Russ, who greets the fatigued chef cordially.

"Hey buddy, I thought you weren't going to be here?"

Miles slightly turns his head when answering. "Yeah, decided to come in."

Russ takes a spot next to Miles, getting ready to prep food when he catches a glimpse of Miles' cutting board. It's soaked in blood.

"Dude!"

Miles looks down and sees the crimson mess for himself. Not only that, but mingled in with the tomatoes and blood sits the tip of his finger, almost ready to dice. Suddenly Miles feels the pain. His wince is a mixture of panic, ache, and exhaustion combined into one.

Russ' glance darts around uneasily. "Dude what the fuck!" He spots a towel and hastily grabs it. "Man, we don't want Darin seeing this!"

But the moment Darin's name is mentioned, there he is, strolling through the swinging doors. "Hey has anyone seen a clip board around here? And I heard my name. What's up?"

Russ answers, "Oh we were just talking about tomorrow, telling Miles about the big crowd we were expecting."

Chapter VIII

"Oh," Darin replies. He then catches a glimpse of the floor near Miles. "Hey man, you're getting tomato juice all over the floor. You should be finished by now cutting everything up."

Russ now has a slight smirk on his face. *Yup, cutting 'everything' up alright.*

Miles can only posture through the pain. "I need to go home. Not feeling very well at all right now."

Darin now sees the blood-soaked towel on the floor. A look of disgust appears on his face. "Okay… but give me a minute to finish some paperwork and I'll finish up what you started."

Russ tries hard not to throw out some smart assed comment or two, reminding himself, *Keep your cool man. This is good stuff here.*

Darin promptly returns to the back office. "Man that was close," Russ sighs in relief.

Miles queasily requests of Russ, "Let me use your cell. Need to call a friend to fix me up."

"Sure man, and I'll clean up here and finish cutting tomatoes for you."

Miles doesn't trust Russ, but has limited options. "Please Russ, clean up thoroughly, you know what I mean?"

"Sure man. Not a drop of blood. Gonna be kinda hard tomato juice being so close to the same color of blood and all." Russ starts to hand Miles the phone. "Uh, you *will* use the other hand, right?"

Miles nods. Right now Miles has no choice but to trust Russ, and rushes off to the bathroom to call Eric again to the rescue. After a minute or so in the bathroom, Miles suddenly remembers something. "Oh shit! Russ!" Miles hastily wraps a wad of paper towel over the blood-soaked real towel around his hand and rushes back into the kitchen, where Russ is chopping away. The smell of onions hangs in the air. "Russ!" Miles whisper-yells.

Russ is startled, quickly turning around with a blank look on his face.

"Hey man, I left the tip of my finger on the cutting board."

Russ inspects Miles and the blood-soaked wrap on his hand, seeing that it is once again starting to drip. "Dude! I just cleaned up the floor!"

His finger throbbing as he imagines the worst, Miles wonders if he could be mistaken. No! It's definitely here. Russ grimaces slightly as he reaches into his back pocket pulls out a ball of foil, handing it to Miles.

Is that my—What the hell was he going to do with it? Miles thinks, but simply shakes his head. "Hey, get me a plastic bag with ice in it."

Russ finds a baggie but has to go outside to the ice machine. He quickly comes back, opens the ice baggie and lets Miles drop his finger tip in it. The still astonished colleague turns away a little as the gruesome object falls in.

Miles heads for the door, but turns around to thank Russ.

"Any time man, any time."

Back in the bathroom, Miles unwraps his hand and rewraps it with a fresh towel. There it occurs to him why he's bleeding so much. It's because of his liver disease from so much heavy drinking. Just lovely. He removes his cell phone from his pocket to get Eric's number, and sets it on top of the sink. Next he gets a decent grip on Russ's phone in his right hand and dials the number. Again, it's the same thing: If Eric can't identify the number, he probably won't answer. That's exactly what happens.

Again Miles leaves a message on Eric's voice mail, "Dude give me a call back at this number, it's Miles. I got an emergency, I cut the tip of my finger off and its bleeding like hell. I'm—"

The beep of the voice mail cuts Miles off. Frustrated and in pain, Miles waits for Eric's call back. In no time the cell phone rings, and Miles

Chapter VIII

answers.

"Dude *what's* going on now?"

Miles is now in a panic, "I cut the tip of my finger off and I'm bleeding like hell. I'm at work in the restroom. Can you help me out man?"

"Shit man, I'm busy. Can't you get one of your co-workers to take you to the emergency room?"

"Man please!" Miles begs.

"DAMN IT, Miles! Okay, okay. I'm on my way. Keep pressure on it." Eric immediately begins considering the worst: Reattaching the tip of Miles' finger. Timing. Miles passing out or something. Blood everywhere.

Miles thinks about telling Eric *I owe you one*, but instead just says "Thanks." After hanging up, he hunches over the sink for no more than a few seconds before there is a knock on the door. Miles gives an annoyed and groggy exhale, "Gonna be a while. Not. feeling. well." *There's another restroom around the corner so, whoever it is…*

Miles looks down at the towel and again finds his hand getting soaked with blood. He is now even less sure about what happens next, and can only tell himself, *Hurry up, Eric!*

Not long after, there is another knock on the door. Miles lets out a frustrated "Hey not feeling—"

"Miles it's Eric."

Miles gives a relieved sigh and opens the door.

Eric gets right to the point, "Ok Miles as you know you are going to need stitches, but I don't have access to do the proper equipment for this procedure, so for right now we're just going to have to apply a pressure pack to it. I'd rather take care of this at your place than here."

Miles gives a compliant "Ok."

"Let's wrap this again. I don't want you bleeding all over my car."

As Miles and Eric exit the bathroom, the guy who must have been the one knocking eyes the two and mouths to Miles, "No wonder." Miles catches the look. *That guy thinks me and Eric are together.* Since Eric had entered the restroom, however, Miles hadn't really looked at Eric's face. Until now. Eric is wearing makeup. Eyeliner, no less!

Eric sees Miles' gawking expression. "What's wrong with you?"

Miles' mouth gyrates and puppets oddly as no words come out for the first second, until it finally finds sound. "Can you give this cell phone back to Russ for me? He's in the kitchen." Miles hands the cell to Eric with his right hand, keeping the gloved hand suspiciously tucked away like a broken paw. He continues heading towards the exit, but can't get the image out of his mind. It doesn't matter though. Of all people, Eric is his friend and always will be.

Eric catches up with Miles and the two start the trip back to Miles' place as soon as Eric removes the eyeliner.

Now in the car, Miles decides to pull his keys from his pocket. As he does, something else falls out. Eric sees it and asks, "What's that? Let me get it for you." While steering, the friend manages to find the mystery item on the passenger floor.

Eric examines the dropped item carefully with one hand on the steering wheel, shifting his gaze back and forth between it and the road. A stern look clouds his face. "Natalie in the hospital. You cutting your finger. It's all about this isn't it?"

Miles is quiet.

Eric easily throws the heroin out the window. The car is currently passing over a bridge, so that the ugly package disappears into the dark background of the flowing creek below. Miles is stunned, but knows Eric is right.

Eric continues, "And when you were staring at me like I was from another planet, we all have secrets and bad habits. But your habit kills. It's

Chapter VIII

killing you both. Think about it Miles."

There is nothing but silence in the car.

Arriving back at home, Miles feels some relief from the pain. Eric parks the car in front of Natalie's parents' house this time, and the two head up the driveway towards the back house. As they approach, however, the front door to the main house opens and a lady steps out. It's Mrs. Ortiz, looking for the cat.

"Hey Miles, I am looking for Lucky. She hasn't come to the door and it's time for her dinner."

Miles thinks to himself, *Just great. Another obstacle.* In a friendly, calm voice Miles replies, "No Mrs. Ortiz. I have not seen her but if I do I will definitely carry her back to you." Not wanting to be rude, Miles also introduces Eric. "And this is my friend Eric. I don't know if Natalie mentioned him to you. He's going to school to be a nurse."

Mrs. Ortiz's face lights up. "You are! Cause I have a pain right here." Natalie's mother beams, pointing to her side.

"Nice to meet you," Eric smiles. "But about that pain, I would check with your physician."

Mrs. Ortiz responds pleasantly, "Okay I will do that. I am not going to keep you boys, but if you see Lucky please bring him to me, not my husband. He's jealous of Lucky."

"Sure, will do that," Miles answers.

As the two continue on to the back house, Mrs. Ortiz calls Miles again. "Miles where's Natalie? I haven't seen her walk by."

Miles' expression flips upside-down. With a long-ish blink and a slight inhale though, he has it fully fixed by the time he turns around. "She's in the apartment sleeping. She wasn't feeling well so she left work early."

"Okay, well let me know how she's doing. If you all need anything, you know where to find me."

"Thank you, Mrs. Ortiz."

By now the blood is dripping from Miles finger onto the grass, not onto the sidewalk.

As soon as Miles and Eric approach the front door, they hear something that sounds like a cat growling. Next comes something from beneath the screen door that looks like a watery substance.

"Oh, shit!" Miles runs to the screen door to open it, and out dashes Lucky the cat.

"Damn man, how long you think he's been there?" Eric frets.

Miles answers somewhat irritated. "Thank God he can't talk. That's what he gets. I must have been so tired I just didn't see him trying to get in the apartment. He must have been there at least five hours, maybe more."

"Hey, my first aid kit is in the car," Eric remembers. "Be right back. Start unwrapping your finger."

Miles goes into the bathroom and starts unwrapping. He hasn't seen his finger since he cut it.

Now down to the last unwrapping, Miles' finger still bleeds without a tip. He remembers the rest of it in his pocket and takes out the watery baggie. Eric enters the bathroom shortly thereafter, and Miles hands the pack to him. Now that the wound is exposed, the pain has become unbearable.

Eric inspects the bag closely, slightly irritated that Miles has handed him another thing with no explanation. "What is this?"

"My fingertip's in there," Miles winces.

Eric sighs and takes the baggie back to the kitchen, where it will sit

Chapter VIII

in the freezer for a while. Soon he returns.

"Look Miles, right now I am going to put a pressure pack on this to stop the bleeding, because too much time has elapsed and reattachment is not an option. But promise me tomorrow you'll go to the emergency room. And don't forget your fingertip." Eric's instructions are clear as he concentrates hard on doctoring Miles' finger. The temporary fix is set in no time.

Eric continues, "Try to keep it level with the heart. And not a lot of movement."

"I will. Thanks man, I will," Miles frowns.

"How is Natalie doing?" Eric asks.

"It was scary at first. She was in ICU, but they moved her to the Medical Surgical floor."

"She is very lucky." Eric hesitates for a while before adding, "You guys really have to stop doing this. It's a warning now."

Miles nods his head.

As soon as Eric is finished, he wishes Miles luck again, then leaves.

Miles stands alone in the bathroom for another minute, thinking to himself, *He's right*.

Miles wakes up suddenly to find a figure standing over him. It's Natalie. Standing angrily in her hospital gown, her IV protruding from her neck, she launches into cold words for the boyfriend. Miles struggles to adjust his eyes, realizing he's not dreaming. "See what you've done to me," she accuses. Instantly she pulls the needle from her neck, blood squirting in different directions. Miles initially freezes, not knowing what to do. Then he reaches up to Natalie's neck to try to stop the bleeding. But as he reaches for her, Natalie disappears.

Miles wakes up soaked in sweat, but not just sweat alone. Somehow the bandage has come off of his finger, and now there is more blood than ever. The dream must have made him that restless. It is 5:00am and too early for the clinic to be open, but he needs to get his finger taken care of. He nervously wraps his finger with the extra gauze that Eric left, and gets dressed. On his way to the door, he remembers the tip of his finger in the fridge. He retrieves it, then heads out again. But first, he gives a quick check before locking the front door, just to make sure Lucky isn't around again.

Chapter IX

A loud noise shakes Natalie from sleep. *What the hell was that!* she works uphill against the meds to pull her thoughts together. Maybe she fell asleep after the shakedown with her roommate. The last thing she remembers is Dee being questioned by that cop.

Pregnant and a user? Natalie keeps trying to get over it. The room is silent now, but still…*What was that noise? Whatever it was, now would be a great time to go to the restroom. Dee is probably sleeping.* Natalie again wishes the restroom was on her side.

Natalie removes the sheet covering her, and observes that she's wearing a gown. Her scarred up legs tell all the story anyone would want to know, and she wonders with more than a little shame what the nurses thought when they saw this. Such an innocent-looking woman. Natalie weakly recalls her previous experience using an IV pump during her time in rehab. Careful not to disturb the IV access in her neck, she unplugs the pump and wraps the plug around it. She quietly walks over to Dee's side, but notices that no one is in the bed.

A tall, slim woman opens the door to the room. She looks at the bed and then at Natalie. "Oh, hi! I am looking for my daughter Dee. Have you seen her?"

Natalie's mouth is a little dry as she speaks. "I just woke up and noticed she wasn't in her bed. She could be in the restroom." Immediately Natalie remembers the loud crash she heard. She and Dee's mother both look over at the restroom door.

Dee's mother turns the knob to open the door. She pushes it, but it seems like something is blocking the way. "Dee are you in there?" the mother calls with caring caution.

There is nothing but silence.

Natalie looks around the room. *Of course she would have to take her pump in there with her.*

Dee's mother puts her ear close to the door, thinking she might have heard something. "Dee are you in there?" she asks again. Again she attempts to push the door, and once again something seems to be blocking it. Suddenly the mother starts to panic, and runs out of the room.

Natalie is at a loss. She only remembers that she had gotten up to use the restroom. Now this. Suddenly Dee's mother returns with two people: her nurse and the same guy in scrubs that Natalie assumes snitched on Dee about the heroin. The two immediately begin pushing on the restroom door, which is soon opened wide enough for the nurse to squeeze in.

GASP! The nurse is alarmed by whatever she sees. "Charles, it's a code blue!"

The guy in scrubs darts out, and quickly returns with two more nurses. They park the gurney outside the door. Now with the door opened wide, Natalie can see Dee sprawled out on the floor. The pump next to her is smashed in. This was the sound that had woken Natalie up. Apparently, Dee had gotten to the syringe inside the pump, probably morphine, and helped herself. Natalie takes two steps back in shock.

The nurses carry Dee's lifeless body to the gurney, where one of them gives her CPR. Dee's mother is hysterical, crying and shaking, such that she needs to be escorted out of the room. The entire calamity unfolds

Chapter IX

in under a minute, but seems to drag out over the course of lifetimes. One for every nurse, every person involved.

Two minutes later, the room is silent again.

Natalie wonders what Dee used to break open the pump. Once in the bathroom, she sees that the pump had been taken off the pole, and the pole then used to smash the pump. The improvised sledgehammer now lay slightly bent on the floor. Soon, Natalie's nurse comes back into the room.

"Natalie I am so sorry you had to see all of this. We are preparing another room for you. Plus we just got orders for you to get a CT scan."

Charles, the nurse's assistant, walks in next, telling both the nurse and Natalie, "There is going to be an investigator up here asking questions on what took place here. They did not give me a time, but just be prepared."

Natalie instantly begins thinking of the worst things that could happen. The investigator will see the tracks on her arms and legs. He'll probably think Natalie had something to do with the incident. She'll be taken in for being a user. They'll call her parents. She wants nothing to do with the legal system.

"We're moving her to another room, and from there she's been put down for a CT scan," Natalie's nurse tells Charles. "So make sure he checks with the front desk before he comes looking for her." Charles nods his head and leaves. Nancy then turns to Natalie, "I'll check to see if your room is ready."

But Natalie is still worried about the investigator. "Reality" unfolds before her. "Okay," she replies. Subtly though, she has already begun the desperate search for a way out.

Natalie finally gets to use the restroom, but wanders off in her own thoughts instead. Soon Nancy has returned.

"Your room is still not ready. Let's gather your things and we can just go down to get your CT scan done. Your room should be ready by the time we get back."

Nancy goes into a small closet and brings out a big plastic bag. Natalie is relieved to realize that her clothes are in it.

"We don't have to take this pump down with us. Let me disconnect the line," the nurse continues. "We shouldn't be gone too long."

Chapter X

Nancy helps Natalie into the wheelchair and starts the two toward the elevator. In Natalie's thinking, *I cannot be questioned by that investigator* is the only idea that makes sense. As they enter the elevator, Natalie asks Nancy a question in order to distract herself.

"Is Dee going to be okay?"

Nancy, though aware of the need for confidentiality, is more likely to talk about the event since Natalie *was* in the room when all of it took place. "It's hard to say. Overdose, but we did get her back. It's touch and go right now."

"And the baby?"

"They had to do an emergency c-section. It was stillborn."

Tears begin to well up in Natalie's eyes upon hearing this, but she continues to talk through it with Nancy. "Dee is very lucky, considering."

"Indeed she is. Indeed she is." Nancy seems to reflect longer on Dee—how she'll react when she finds out about the baby.

Just before the elevator door closes, Natalie notices something on the floor a few feet outside of it. Natalie wastes no time in pointing it out to

Nancy. "Did you drop that?"

Nancy turns around and recognizes the paperwork. "Oh, that's your orders. Hold the door while I get it," she tells Natalie.

Natalie moves the wheelchair forward to hold the door open, but before she can stop it, it closes, almost taking her hand. Meanwhile outside the elevator, Nancy scoops up the papers, "Got it." But turning around to get back on, she catches the last glimpse of her patient as the doors shut. "Great. Just great." The nurse stands there for a while waiting for the elevator to come back up, in the meantime observing that it does indeed go all the way to the basement, where radiology is located.

Nancy hopes for a moment that Natalie got off at the basement level. Then again maybe Natalie didn't know which floor radiology was actually on. She is relieved when, about a minute later, the elevator heads back up. That is, until the elevator doors open. "Fuck." The wheelchair is empty. Nancy boards the elevator and pushes the button to the basement. *She just got out of the wheelchair and she is waiting for me*, she reasons. But who is she kidding? Why would the patient leave an empty wheelchair in the elevator?

Nancy gets off the elevator. No Natalie. She goes through the double doors that lead to radiology and immediately heads to the front desk. Asking the unit clerk if she had seen a patient with dark hair in a gown, Nancy receives the answer she had hoped not to hear. "No." It is now late in the evening so everything is slow. "…but let me check in the waiting room," the clerk adds. "Maybe she slipped by me."

The clerk is only gone for a second. "Sorry, but no one is in there."

"Thanks." Nancy heads back to her unit, more bugged than anything else. *What a way to end my shift. I will do my report, but first have to call security.*

The distorted look on Natalie's face made her seem unreal, even sinister as she stepped off the elevator just two minutes earlier. As she had left her wheelchair with her clothes in hand, she allowed the heavy doors to slowly close behind her. Now she actually has a chance to leave this place, but how will she do it?

Nancy is approached by Charles as soon as she arrives back in Medical Surgical. "Hey, the investigator is here. Where is your patient?"

Where IS she? Tch. She tells Charles, "Don't know. I lost her in the elevator."

"What!?"

"Tell you later, but right now I have to call security. Do me favor and tell the investigator I will be over in a second." Nancy makes her call to security and then heads over to the investigator.

"Hello. I understand you want to ask me some questions?"

"Yes," the serious man confirms stoically. "Now I understand you were the nurse on duty?"

"Yes."

"So were you there at the time she locked herself in the restroom and broke into the pump?"

"Actually sir, I came after the incident, the person you really need to talk to is…not here."

"What do you mean 'not here?'"

Nancy gives a brief summary of what has happened. Before she can finish, however, security arrives at the front desk. Nancy excuses herself from the investigator.

Now the security guard has questions for Nancy. "Are you the one who reported a patient disappearing?"

"Yes," Nancy replies, one hand on her hip in objection to all the trouble these patients are causing.

"I'm going to need a description," the security guard says.

Nancy relays the relevant information.

"So you said she had an IV still connected?" the guard confirms.

Nancy knows right away where this is leading. The police are going to have to get involved since the IV is hospital property that the patient has effectively stolen. Not only that, having an IV still connected is probably like heaven for her patient; as a drug user, all she has to do is apply the needle to the line with the heroin for a constant fix instead of looking for the vein, and Nancy knows that Natalie's veins are shot. Getting back to the security guard's question Nancy answers, "Yes." Sure enough, the guard adjusts his inquiry.

"We are going to have to get the police involved in this since she still has the IV connected. It's considered stolen hospital property."

Nancy nods her head.

"Let me make a call to the police department so they can go ahead and send a car to her house. I am going to need to get her address."

Nancy points to the nurses station and tells the guard, "Talk to our unit clerk. She can get you that information."

The security guard thanks Nancy and goes over to the nurses station.

Now let me finish talking to the investigator, Nancy sighs. She turns back around to where he was, however, to find him gone.

Nancy sees Charles and asks, "What happened to the investigator?"

"He still needed to interview Dee's Mother," Charles replies.

"Is he coming back to talk to me?"

"I don't know."

"It's been a long day. If he's not back up here in the next 30 minutes I am going home."

Chapter X

Charles understands that frustration which often comes with this line of work, "I don't blame you."

Chapter XI

Natalie searches around for a bathroom to change her clothes. She spots one, but to her left sees a sign reading "Radiology." By now she knows that she has been reported missing. She is also sure that, if that investigator talked to her, he would probably think she was in on the thing with Dee because of her own prior use of heroin. When she thinks of this, she wants to kill Miles, *This is why I told him NO HOSPITALS*. Looking both ways, she quickly dashes toward the door.

Natalie grips the knob, but it won't turn. She thinks there might be someone in there, but a lot of the time people will at least make noise or say something. Or maybe the staff lost track of time and forgot to unlock it. All she can think about now is changing clothes and finding the exit.

Walking opposite the direction of radiology, Natalie comes upon a door with no sign. Desperate to get out of the hallway and change her gown, she turns the knob and slips an arm into the pitch black room. It takes some time for her to feel around for a light switch, but once she finds it, she turns it on then immediately turns it back off again. That had been just to see what was in this room. Now she knows it's a supply closet. Still cautiously opening the door as she looks down the hallway, she soon enters fully into the room and closes the door.

The supply closet is nothing but darkness. Natalie continues to feel around, groping various shelves and their objects, but she is too afraid to turn the lights back on, out of concern that someone might see. The nervous patient knows there is a shelf to her right, and reaches for what might be on top. There is nothing useful. The very bottom of the shelf, however, is stacked with bed pans. Given all of the events of the evening, Natalie had forgotten all about needing to use the restroom. Now feeling the pains in her stomach, light headed and unsteady, she can't hold it any longer. She grabs the first bed pan and relieves herself. Once finished, she carefully pushes the pan underneath the shelf to avoid stepping in it.

Now feeling like a completely new person, Natalie takes her clothes out of the plastic bag and gets dressed. The closet is small and awkward, but she manages the feat successfully. Next she searches for anything else she might use, and locates some gauze. The IV in her neck is further secured, then she takes her hair out of its ponytail. *Thank God*, she thinks, for the long hair which covers her neck perfectly.

Natalie's next aim is to find an exit through the maze of hallways before her. The hospital is, of course, a big place, so that it seems as though every exit you go through just leads to another exit. She cracks open the door, but all of a sudden hears footsteps. The door is quickly closed again, but not before Natalie's heel kicks something over as she backs up. Still in the dark, she stoops over to feel what the item was. The wetness on the floor immediately tells her *exactly* what it was. Natalie tries to keep quiet, sweeping her feet to prevent the spill from seeping under the door, but is unsuccessful. At the same time, one of the voices attached to the footsteps stops right there. Natalie presses her ear to the door and listens. There are two male voices.

"I appreciate you letting me come down here this late to say goodbye to her," the first man says.

"No problem, the only number she had on her person was yours," says the other.

"Well I don't want to keep you. I know you are a very busy man."

"Alright, you can either take the elevator, which is to the left, or the

Chapter XI

stairs, straight ahead to the right."

"Thank you again," the first man replies.

"Don't forget. First right, hang a left."

"Thank you."

Silence follows. Outside the door, however, the second man—dressed in scrubs—must have looked down. "What is this?" he observes some sort of spillage on the floor. As the knob turns, Natalie simultaneously locks the door from the inside. Again there are footsteps as the man leaves. Unfortunately, Natalie can't make out the last part of what this person said. Her panic goes through the roof. It could be the hospital police.

The man in scrubs and one of the housekeeping staff show up at the supply closet door less than a minute later. "Watch your step," the former tells the latter as both of them inspect the spillage.

The housekeeper attempts to unlock the door, but instead ends up locking it. Turning around towards the man in scrubs she notes, "Sir this door is open." She takes her keys and unlocks the door again, cautiously opening it. She soon finds the light switch and turns on the light.

The supply closet door is now completely opened, where the only objects to be found are linens, towels, and housekeeping supplies. The housekeeper and staff member look down at the floor again. There is no sign of any spillage, so the man in scrubs bends down and touches the wet substance outside of the door with his finger. He then puts it to his nose and smells it. Puts his finger to his tongue and tastes it. The housekeeper is disgusted, but clearly curious. "Well what is it?"

The staff member dips his finger into the small pool and tastes it again. "That's what I thought it was. With all the medicines mixed in it, it's urine."

The housekeeper's jaw drops open.

Natalie climbs the stairs with a faint and weakly trudge. Finally arriving at a sign reading "1ˢᵗ Floor," she creeps through the featureless door and into a deserted hallway. One thing is certain: It's very late. As she travels the hall, Natalie reminds herself repeatedly, *Remain normal. If somebody asks questions just say you got an emergency call from a relative.*

On her left, Natalie spots a gift shop, another waiting area, then finally an exit sign. Her escape, though, is interrupted by a pair of voices coming her way. *Remain calm.* The voices are getting closer, but Natalie sees a sign for the hospital chapel just in time.

Two men round the corner before Natalie can get inside of the chapel. Immediately she buries her face in one hand and begins crying.

"Are you okay?" one of the men asks.

Natalie responds tearfully. "Just a relative. I have to go and pray for her." The pretend-distraught escapee heads straight for the chapel door. One on the men even opens it for her.

"Allow me."

"Thank you," Natalie sobs, still covering her mouth.

"You are so very welcome," the man replies. He then closes the door behind her.

Once inside the chapel, Natalie backs up a little and looks around. There is someone sitting in the back row, the presence of whom startles her, so she goes to the other side of the small chapel and takes a seat in one of the pews. Natalie is exhausted by now. She is so thankful to finally get a chance to sit and get some much-needed rest. Straight ahead, a small altar invites her stare as she wonders what she has done to deserve all of this. But why question? The last thing she needs is more complication.

Glancing across the aisle, one can see that the gentleman there is motionless. *It's a weird time to go,* Natalie thinks, since she still needs to

Chapter XI

play the role of the grieving relative. She makes the sign of the cross, kneels, and starts praying. *Maybe I should have been doing this all along. Maybe I wouldn't be in this predicament.* Finally having come to reason with herself, Natalie makes the sign of the cross again and gets up. Knowing the other person is still there, she prepares a friendly smile before leaving. But no one is there when she turns around. Natalie wonders why she didn't hear anything when the man left. Nevermind, it's time to go.

Natalie carefully opens the chapel door, trying to avoid looking suspicious. She walks out, and has no trouble finding the exit sign. She doesn't want the main lobby, of course. She needs the parking garage. *Yes!* She soon finds the directions she needs. Suddenly Natalie begins to feel sick again, and looks down at her hands. They are shaking from all of the evading she's had to do. Putting on her best normal walk, she finally arrives at the double exit doors, which automatically open for her. An ocean of pavement and a few quiet cars greet her. Natalie never knew the smell of a parking garage could be so heavenly.

Chapter XII

    Natalie feels progressively weaker even as she gets beyond the hospital. She takes a seat on a cement bench and hunches over, now concerned with how she is going to get home. She has no money for a taxi. The buses aren't running. Suddenly a pair of shoes appear before her, prompting her to raise her head. There stands a man in dark pants and dark shirt—whether black or maybe night blue, she cannot not tell—and whose features are a blur. Natalie immediately recognizes him as security.

    "Miss are you waiting for someone?" The man's tone is deep, serious.

    Natalie doesn't have time to answer before a car stops nearby. The driver peeps his head through the passenger window. "Sir I am looking for a—"

    The security guard moves from in front of Natalie, allowing the driver to see her. Immediately, the driver begins a conversation of his own.

    "Emily, I was looking all over for you!"

    "Sir, do you know this person?" the guard inquires.

    "Yes, she is a friend of mine. We came here to visit her relative and

I told her to wait down here while I get the car," the unknown driver explains.

Natalie's only option seems to be to play along with the story, but should she? "Joe I am sorry I got light headed and needed some fresh air." Natalie gets up normally and walks to the car. Nervously she takes a seat on the passenger side.

The driver peeps his head out again, but with Natalie in the passenger seat, he tries not to get too close to her. "Thank you, sir," he says to the security guard. The guard has no reply, but keeps a stern frown glued to his face until he is no longer the main feature in the rearview mirror.

The car is not yet out of the parking garage when the mystery driver asks Natalie, "Do you always get into cars with strangers?" his eyes remain fixed straight ahead. The sound of the automatic car lock sends chills through Natalie's body, moving her to clutch her arms in protection.

"I know most of the security people that work here at the hospital," the driver says, "but him I do not recognize."

Natalie begins to shiver quietly. Her thoughts are unfocused. *What am I doing? Why is he talking about security? He's a stranger. I should have stayed with the guard.* The nervous young woman timidly requests, "Can you please let me out?"

"Do you want me to take you to your car?" the driver asks.

But Natalie knows she has no car. She is hesitant, but *why would he offer that? Maybe he's not a bad guy.*

"Look I don't mind taking you to your car. Or home after seeing how shaken you were in the chapel."

Natalie freezes, then turns her head to get a better look at him. "That was you?"

Chapter XII

The driver turns to Natalie, "Yes."

Almost out of the parking garage, Natalie suddenly spots another security guard, this time right in front of the driver's oncoming car. Just in time she yells, "Watch Out!"

When the driver turns to look ahead, however, there is nothing there. Natalie instantly realizes it was her imagination. "Sorry, I'm tired."

Now thinking about her maneuvers in the chapel, Natalie tries to get back into character, grieving again. "Yes, I'm still a little shaken up. If it's not out of your way I would be glad if you could take me home." Natalie then gives the man her address and directions.

The car is so silent, Natalie eventually attempts to break the ice by asking who the man was praying for in the chapel. At first he seems reluctant to talk about it.

In flashback, the stranger could not get the image out of his mind. The way she just lie there motionless. He remembers when he first met her. She was troubled, just someone thrown out on the street as a young girl, and prostitution was her only source of income. The things that came with the street life were what you would expect: drugs, exploitation, and different kinds of crime. Before he went into ministry he had lived under similar circumstances, found in a ditch with a needle stuck in his arm as the blood oozed out. He recalls being locked up in a room for what seemed like forever, for his own safety they said, to get over his addiction. When he got the call to come down to the hospital to identify a body, he knew it was her. Apparently, his phone number was the only number she had on her. And as he looked at the motionless body, he covered the mark on her forehead—the one that she had injected with drugs—with some of her hair. It was over, but still he bent down and gave her a kiss saying, "You are free now." To Natalie he described her simply as "…a friend that I have been helping. But I guess it wasn't enough." Then he turned the question over to Natalie herself. What was her purpose?

Natalie substitutes her hospital roommate for the reason. "My cousin who is eight months pregnant, had some difficulties with drugs. So that's the reason why."

The driver can only shake his head. "Drugs are a terrible thing. Thank God I was strong enough."

The trip back home flies by, and before Natalie knows it she is back in front of her parents' house. She can't believe how quickly they arrived.

"Well, here we are," the driver announces. "Your car should be okay at the hospital garage."

In that moment, Natalie suddenly forgets all of the pain and weakness from earlier. Instead, she actually feels rejuvenated in some way. She gets out of the car, and before closing the door, turns back to the driver with a sincere "Thank you." The man nods, Natalie closes the door, and he drives away.

There was something about him, Natalie thinks, *but what?* Then, while proceeding down her parents' walkway, she suddenly turns around and looks back down the street. *The voice!* That was him outside the door

Chapter XII

in the hospital when she was in the supply room. She stands in silence for a few seconds before moving on.

Natalie is now more carefree than she has been in a long time, strolling down her parents' walkway. She has no idea what time it is, but knows that it's late.

Chapter XIII

    Miles had been in a deep sleep for some time, but then woke up thinking about what he had accomplished that morning. He had gone to the clinic, gotten stitches in his finger, but now looked at his fingertip in a small jar. It turns out that they couldn't reattach it. Instead of buying more drugs, he had paid the cell phone bill. So now he has service again. All day he had wanted to call the hospital to check on Natalie, but had kept deciding against it. He did not want to upset her. After some time in thought, he quickly dozes off again.

    Suddenly Miles awakens to a figure standing over him. He shakes into alertness, immediately getting his senses together, *Not another dream.*

    "Miles! Miles, wake up! Wake up!" Natalie kicks the bed. "Get the stuff ready." She then removes the gauze from her neck with the IV dangling from it.

    Miles flies out of bed. This isn't a dream.

    Natalie repeats, "Get the stuff."

    But Miles knows Natalie is not going to like what she's about to hear. "I don't have any."

Natalie is instantly enraged. "You used it all up!"

Miles hangs his head down, delicately breaking the news. "I threw it out the window." He knows full well that Eric did it, *but what does it matter? Damn it Eric!*

Natalie is now out of control, "How could you!"

Miles hopes this next fit will be quick. Hopefully she'll calm down.

Miles tries to reason with Natalie in a low voice, "First, keep it down. We don't want to wake up your parents."

Natalie starts shaking, but tries hard to keep it together. Still out of control, she commands Miles, "Go get some, NNNOWWW!" she growls.

Miles, though usually composed, has finally had enough as he realizes that Natalie probably wasn't officially released from the hospital. "Natalie how the hell did you get out of the hospital? How did you get here!?"

Natalie remains furious, "Look you put me in the hospital when I told you not to! Now you throw my shit out!? What the FUCK!"

"Well Natalie since you masterminded some great escape—I don't know how you did it—but wouldn't you think this place would be surrounded by cops right now? Cause I gave them a fake address. It was for you! They won't follow you! They won't know! You were DYING, babe!"

Natalie's glare lords over Miles, cold and angry, with not so much as a blinking eye. Miles leaves the room and comes back with a bucket full of empty needles. Dry blood clogs the syringes as the rotten smell chokes the room. He tilts the bucket and shows it to Natalie. Then he points at the mattress on the floor. There is no bed frame, just a mattress. "Baby look how we're living! Dogs live better than this!"

Miles moves closer to Natalie and lovingly takes her in his arms. "Don't you want to be able to wear short sleeves again?" He slowly pulls his beloved near, and holds her.

Chapter XIII

While holding her, Miles did not feel the blood dripping down his back, seeping down his white t-shirt.

Natalie had her IV in her hand.

www.ingramcontent.com/pod-product-compliance
Lightning Source LLC
Chambersburg PA
CBHW030457010526
44118CB00011B/976